KEKICH'S CREDOS

~ 100 Credos to Live By ~

By Dave Kekich

Presented by David A. Streen

KEKICH'S CREDOS

~ 100 Credos to Live By ~

By Dave Kekich

Presented by:
David A. Streen

Illustrations by Skye Streen

KEKICH'S CREDOS Intro
100 Credos to Live By

"On the following pages are Kekich's Credos, which consist of 100 "success secrets" that my good friend Dave Kekich wrote and compiled as a result of his life experiences. They are priceless. Reading and applying them every day will give you insight, clarity, and a positive effect in every aspect of your life... from your business to your personal life."

-Joe Polish, Founder of Genius Network®

"Learning these Credos will change your life, applying them could change the world!"

-Dave Streen, Founder of We Help Authors™

Contents

ANNUAL KEKICH CREDOS
LIVE ZOOM

Once a year we host a live Kekich Credos Zoom session.

It is simple:
We go through the Credos, talk about what actually works in real life, and do live Q&A.

If you want an invitation, join the notification list.

JOIN HERE:

WeHelpAuthors.com/credos

Comfort Zones
KEKICH'S CREDO #1

People will do almost anything to stay in their comfort zones. If you want to accomplish anything, get out of your comfort zone. Strive to increase order and discipline in your life. Discipline usually means doing the opposite of what you feel like doing. The easy roads to discipline are 1) setting deadlines, 2) discovering and doing what you do best and what's important and enjoyable to you, and 3) focusing on habits by replacing your bad habits and thought patterns, one-by-one, over time, with good habits and thought patterns.

Time
KEKICH'S CREDO #2

Cherish time - your most valuable resource. Invest more and spend less of it. You can never make up the time you lose. It's the most important value for any productive, happy individual and is the only limitation to all accomplishment. To waste time is to waste your life. The most important choices you'll ever make are how you use your time.

Pause and Think
KEKICH'S CREDO #3

Think carefully before making any offers, commitments, or promises, no matter how seemingly trivial. These are contracts and must be honored. These also include self-resolutions.

Results – Life is Easy...
KEKICH'S CREDO #4

Real regrets only come from not doing your best. All else is out of your control. You're measured by results only. Trade excuses and "trying" for results, and expect half-hearted results from half-hearted efforts. Do more than is expected of you. Life's easy when you live it the hard way... and hard if you try to live it the easy way.

Life Gives to the Giver
KEKICH'S CREDO #5

Life gives to the giver and takes from the taker. Always show gratitude when earned, monetarily when possible.

Joe Polish wrote an entire book based on this Credo!

He gives it away for FREE!
Visit **JoesFreeBook.com** *to grab your copy.*

Produce and Save
KEKICH'S CREDO #6

Produce for wealth creation and accumulation. Invest profits for wealth preservation and growth. Produce more than you consume and save a minimum of 20% of all earnings. Pay yourself first.

Success
KEKICH'S CREDO #7

You're successful when you like who and what you are. Success includes achievement... while choosing and directing your own activities. It means enjoying intimate relationships and loving what you do in life.

Giants
KEKICH'S CREDO #8

L earn from the giants.

Insurance and Caution
KEKICH'S CREDO #9

A little caution avoids great regrets. Expect the best and prepare for the worst. Keep fully insured physically and materially and keep hedged emotionally. Insurance is not for sale when you need it.

Competition
KEKICH'S CREDO #10

Out-think, out-innovate and out-hustle the competition, and vividly visualize yourself as winning before entering into every deal or competitive situation. Maintain a blood-smelling, fighter pilot life-or-death attitude when any deal gets near to a win/win close. Learn the other side's needs and character before moving forward. Never underestimate your opposition, and never show weakness when negotiating.

Plan

KEKICH'S CREDO #11

Never enter into nor invest in a business without a solid, well-researched, and well thought-out written plan. Execute the plan with passion and precision. Replace second guessing and wishing with learning and planning. Plan and manage your life the same way.

Ask Focused Questions
KEKICH'S CREDO #12

S uccess comes quickly to those who develop great powers of intense sustained concentration. The first rule is to get involved by asking focused questions.

Protect Your Downside
KEKICH'S CREDO #13

Protect your downside. The upside will take care of itself. Cut your losses short - and let your profits run. This takes tremendous discipline.

Marketing and Innovation
KEKICH'S CREDO #14

The primary purpose of business is to create and keep customers. Marketing and innovation produce results. All other business functions are costs. Prospecting and increasing the average value and frequency of sales are the bedrock of marketing and business.

Reinforce and Reward
KEKICH'S CREDO #15

If it's not proprietary, it won't work. Pay only on performance. Proprietary interest is one of the most powerful forces ever known. Whatever you reinforce or reward, you get more of.

Guarantees
KEKICH'S CREDO #16

Competence starts with guaranteeing your work.

Swim Against the Stream
KEKICH'S CREDO #17

Life operates in reverse action to entropy. Therefore the universe is hostile to life. Progress is a continued effort to swim against the stream.

Do More of What Works
KEKICH'S CREDO #18

Find out what works and then do more of it. Focus first on doing the right things, and then on doing things right by mastering details. A few basic moves produce most results and income.

Leverage, Leverage, Leverage
KEKICH'S CREDO #19

Use leverage with ideas (the ability to generalize is the key to intellectual leverage), work, money, time, and people. To maximize profits, replicate yourself. Earning potentials become geometric rather than linear.

Don't Rationalize
KEKICH'S CREDO #20

Rationalizations are generally convenient evasions of reality and are used as excuses for dishonest behavior, mistakes, and/or laziness.

Achieve or Die
KEKICH'S CREDO #21

Always have lofty explicit goals and visualize them intensely. Assume the attitude that if you don't reach your goals, you will literally die! This type of gun-to-your-head forced focus... survival pressure mindset, no matter how briefly used, stimulates your mind, forces you to use your time effectively... and illuminates new ways of getting things done.

Get Paid Up Front
KEKICH'S CREDO #22

The value of any service you have to offer diminishes rapidly once it's provided. Protect your compensation before performing.

Celebrate Existence
KEKICH'S CREDO #23

Incalculable effort and hardship over countless generations evolved into the life, values, and happiness we take for granted today. Every day should be a celebration of existence. You are a masterpiece of life and should feel and appreciate this all the way down to your bones. Aspire to create, achieve and build onto the great value momentum taking place all around you.

Be Enthusiastic
KEKICH'S CREDO #24

Enthusiasm covers many deficiencies - and will make others want to associate with you.

Be Your Own Boss
KEKICH'S CREDO #25

Working for someone else gives you little chance to make a fortune. By owning your own business, you only have to be good to become wealthy.

Million Dollar Racehorse
KEKICH'S CREDO #26

Religiously nourish your body with proper nutrition, exercise, recreation, sleep and relaxation techniques.

Reach Your Full Potential
KEKICH'S CREDO #27

The choice to exert integrated effort or to default to camouflaged laziness is the key choice that determines your character, competence, and future. That critical choice must be made continually - throughout life. The most meaningful thing to live for is reaching your full potential.

Always Be Growing
KEKICH'S CREDO #28

Keep an active mind and continue to grow intellectually. You either grow or regress. Nothing stands still.

Communicate Clearly
KEKICH'S CREDO #29

Most accomplishment (and problem avoidance) is built on clear persuasive communication. That includes knowing each other's definitions, careful listening, thinking before talking, focused questioning, and observing your feedback. Become a communications expert.

Take Full Control
KEKICH'S CREDO #30

Power comes from stripping away appearances and seeing things as they really are. Socialism appeals to psychological and intellectual weaklings. Identify and replace all external authorities with internal strength and competence. Take full control of, and responsibility for, your conscious mind and every aspect of your life. Being incompetent in any part of your life or business or being dependent on an unproven person opens you up to sloppiness, manipulation, and irrationality.

Be Honest, Always
KEKICH'S CREDO #31

If there is not a conscious struggle to be honest in difficult situations, you are probably being dishonest. Characters aren't really tested until things aren't going well or until the stakes are high.

Ask For What You Want
KEKICH'S CREDO #32

Do not compromise if you are right. Hold your ground, show no fear, ask for what you want and the opposition will usually agree.

Long Term Outlook
KEKICH'S CREDO #33

If the situation is not right in the long term, walk away from it. Maintain a long term outlook in all endeavors. Live like you don't have much time left... but plan as if you'll live for centuries.

Do Due Diligence
KEKICH'S CREDO #34

Invest only after strict and complete due diligence. Don't allow yourself to be rushed. Make important decisions carefully, consider your gut feelings... then pull the trigger.

Stress Kills
KEKICH'S CREDO #35

Stress kills. No matter how painful in the short-term, remove all chronically stressful situations, environments, and people from your life.

Low Overhead
KEKICH'S CREDO #36

Keep your overhead to a minimum. Rely more on brains, wit and talent... and less on money.

Essences of Business
KEKICH'S CREDO #37

Business is the highest evolution of consciousness and morality. The essences of business are: honesty, effort, responsibility, integration, creativity, objectivity, long-range planning, intensity, effectiveness, discipline, thought, and control. Business is life on all levels at all times.

No Free Lunch
KEKICH'S CREDO #38

That which is most satisfying is that which is earned. Anything received free of charge is seldom valued. You can't get something for (from) nothing. The price is too high.

Strong Philosophy
KEKICH'S CREDO #39

By adhering to a strong honest philosophy, you will remain guiltless, blameless, independent, and maintain control over your life. Without a sound philosophy, your life will eventually crumble.

Have Massive Dreams
KEKICH'S CREDO #40

No dream is too big. It takes almost the same amount of time and energy to manage tiny projects or businesses as it does to manage massive ones... and the massive ones carry with them - proportional rewards.

Avoid Liars and Lying
KEKICH'S CREDO #41

There is no such thing as "just a little theft" or "just a little dishonesty." If someone lies to you once, he'll lie to you a thousand times. Lying is for thieves and cowards.

Be a Good Example
KEKICH'S CREDO #42

L ead by example.

Take Responsibility
KEKICH'S CREDO #43

Take full responsibility for your actions or lack of action. They all have consequences. He who errs must pay. This is an easy concept to grasp from the recipient's end.

Thinking Time - 20 Solutions
KEKICH'S CREDO #44

An hour of effective, precise, hard, disciplined - and integrated thinking can be worth a month of hard work. Thinking is the very essence of, and the most difficult thing to do in business and in life. Empire builders spend hour-after-hour on mental work... while others party. If you're not consciously aware of putting forth the effort to exert self-guided integrated thinking... if you don't act beyond your feelings and instead take the path of least resistance, then you give in to laziness, make bad decisions and no longer control your life. The most powerful way to do this is to insulate yourself from all distractions. Then write a problem or goal on a sheet of paper and force yourself to come up with at least 20 ways to solve your problem or reach your goal. The last solutions are the toughest and are usually the most life changing. Make this exercise a life-long habit.

Who To Take Advice From
KEKICH'S CREDO #45

Only take advice only from people with a history of success in the subject in which you seek advice.

Show Them How To Treat You
KEKICH'S CREDO #46

F irst impressions are lasting impressions. Put your best foot forward. People treat you like you teach them to treat you. A success key is positioning yourself at the top of their agenda.

Do The Right Thing
KEKICH'S CREDO #47

The right thing is usually not the easy thing to do. You may sacrifice popularity for rightness, but you'll lose self-esteem for wrongness. Don't be afraid to say "no."

Sell the Want - Give the Need
KEKICH'S CREDO #48

S ell people what they want, give them what they need.

Respect Other's Property
KEKICH'S CREDO #49

Have strict and total respect for other people's property.

Understand the Other Person
KEKICH'S CREDO #50

P roducing results is more important than proving you're right. To get things done, try to understand others' frames of references, points of view, needs, and wants. Then determine what is honest, fair, effective, and rational... and act accordingly.

Who Do You Spend Time With?
KEKICH'S CREDO #51

Long term success is built on credibility and on establishing enduring loving relationships with quality people based on mutually earned trust. Cut all ties with dishonest, negative or lazy people, and associate with people who share your values. You become whom you associate with.

Don't Control, Manage
KEKICH'S CREDO #52

Outside of yourself, you control nothing... but you can manage anything. Don't be preoccupied with things over which you have no control, and don't take things personally.

Work On - Not In
KEKICH'S CREDO #53

S pend more time working "on" your business than "in" your business.

Long Term Track Record
KEKICH'S CREDO #54

Don't enter into a business relationship with anyone unknown to you without being furnished with references dating back at least 10 years. If he doesn't have good enduring relationships, stay away. Check all representations on which you will rely made by everyone.

Seldom as Good or Bad...
KEKICH'S CREDO #55

Enjoy life. Treat it as an adventure. Care passionately about the outcome, but keep it in perspective. Things are seldom as bleak as they seem when they are going wrong - or as good as they seem when they are going well. Lighten up. You'll live longer.

Identify What You Want
KEKICH'S CREDO #56

Identify exactly what it is you want. This takes a lot of thought. Then don't let anything stand in your way of getting it.

Get Any Job Done
KEKICH'S CREDO #57

You can get any job done through the sheer force of will when combined with uncompromising integrity and competence. Strong leadership is the key.

React Well
KEKICH'S CREDO #58

You are responsible for exactly who, what and where you are in life. That will be just as true this time next year. Situations aren't important. How you react to them is. You have to play it where it lies.

Have Intense Desire
KEKICH'S CREDO #59

The foundation of achievement is intense desire. The world's highest achievers have the highest levels of dissatisfaction. Those with the lowest levels are the failures. The best way to build desire is to make resolute choices for the future.

Integrate Every Aspect
KEKICH'S CREDO #60

Integrate every aspect of your life (body, mind, spirit, relationships, business) and each within itself. Integrating means understanding and digesting a process... and seeing relationships among seemingly unrelated phenomena. It's a sign of innovative genius.

Never Be Deceptive
KEKICH'S CREDO #61

Never be deceptive when trying to achieve a personal gain. Shortchanging others results in loss of self-esteem.

Security Sets the Bar Too Low
KEKICH'S CREDO #62

If your purpose of life is security, you will be a failure. Security is the lowest form of happiness.

All Parties Must Benefit
KEKICH'S CREDO #63

Never enter into a contract unless all parties benefit. But no partnership is ever 50/50. There will always be inequities.

Annually Review the Basics
KEKICH'S CREDO #64

Review the basics of your profession at least once per year.

Move On
KEKICH'S CREDO #65

Bitterness, jealousy, and anger empower your enemies and enslave you. Negative thinking results in the destruction of property. It is anti-property, therefore anti-capitalistic and anti-life. It also erodes your health. Put things behind you, learn your lessons, and get on with your life.

Unique Ability® or Delegate It
KEKICH'S CREDO #66

Most people spend 90% of their time on what they're not best at and what they don't like doing - and only 10% of their time on their best and most enjoyable ability. Geniuses delegate the 90%... and spend all their time on their "unique ability."

"Unique Ability" is a registered trademark of

The Strategic Coach, Inc

You can learn more here:

UniqueAbility.com

and

StrategicCoach.com

High Self-esteem
KEKICH'S CREDO #67

High self-esteem can only come from moral productivity and achievement.

Endless Opportunities
KEKICH'S CREDO #68

There are an infinite number of new opportunities. Actively seek them out, and position yourself to recognize and take advantage of them.

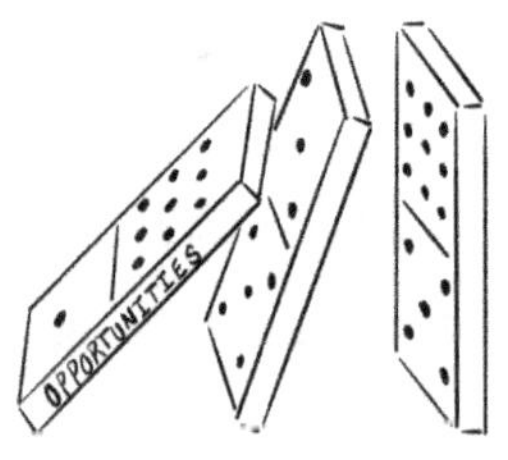

Develop and Utilize Ideas
KEKICH'S CREDO #69

The best way to have good ideas is to have lots of ideas. But there is no such thing as a good idea unless it is developed and utilized. Ditto for prospects.

Maximize Profits
KEKICH'S CREDO #70

For maximum profits, identify and market universal needs, wants and trends. Creating desire, satisfying needs and wants, and replacing problems with creative innovations are the essence of profit generation.

Maximize Opportunities
KEKICH'S CREDO #71

To maximize opportunities, seek and master the complicated. The major solutions you find will be surprisingly simple, and the competition is minimal.

Options and Power
KEKICH'S CREDO #72

Always have options. Options are a primary source of power. Power also comes from stripping away appearances and seeing things as they really are.

Superior Preparation
KEKICH'S CREDO #73

Nothing wins more often than superior preparation. Genius is usually preparation.

Patience is Profitable
KEKICH'S CREDO #74

Patience is profitable. Achievement comes from the sum of consistent small efforts, repeated daily.

Be Persistent
KEKICH'S CREDO #75

Persistence is a sure path to success with quality activities. Never, ever, ever give up.

I Will Do This!
KEKICH'S CREDO #76

"I will do this" is the only attitude that works. "I'll try" or "I think" doesn't. So eliminate "try" from your vocabulary. Unless it violates physical laws, NOTHING is impossible. If you want it badly enough, you can have it.

Bigger Pies
KEKICH'S CREDO #77

Always work on increasing the size of the pie, rather than just your portion.

Take Good Risks
KEKICH'S CREDO #78

Rewards are rare without risks, but take only carefully calculated risks. Make sure the odds are on your side.

How > What
KEKICH'S CREDO #79

The "how" you get it (with integrity) is more important than the "what."

Put It In Writing
KEKICH'S CREDO #80

Be explicit and semantically precise in all communications, agreements and dealings. Summarize and write down important discussions... and make sure all sides agree. Putting agreements in writing avoids misunderstandings. Memories are fallible, and death is inevitable (so far).

Act Now... Get Started
KEKICH'S CREDO #81

The best way to get started is to get started. Life rewards action... not reaction. Wait for nothing. Attack life. Don't plan to death or ask for permission... but act now... and apologize later.

Question Everything
KEKICH'S CREDO #82

Question everything. Don't believe it's true or right just because it's conventional. Strip all limits from your imagination on every deal and look for an unconventional creative opportunity in every mistake, crisis, or problem. Be flexible, and be willing to turn on a dime when advantageous.

What Excites You?
KEKICH'S CREDO #83

Have fun. The single key to a successful happy life is finding a vocation you enjoy - one that excites you the most.

You Will Get Old
KEKICH'S CREDO #84

Nobody gets old by surprise.

Produce More
KEKICH'S CREDO #85

When it's a matter of producing or starving, people don't starve.

Have Great Expectations
KEKICH'S CREDO #86

You get what you expect, not what you want. Fill your life with positive expectations. Demand the best. Attitude and desire contribute to 90% of your achievement. Anyone can learn the physical mechanics.

Add Value to Others
KEKICH'S CREDO #87

The surest way to accomplish your business and personal goals is making service to others your primary goal. The key to success is adding value to others' lives. Success unshared is failure.

Producing > Consumption
KEKICH'S CREDO #88

The source of lasting happiness can never come from outside yourself through consuming values - but only from within yourself by creating values. Producing more than you consume is the only justification for existence.

Attack Fear
KEKICH'S CREDO #89

Unattended problems will not go away, but will usually get worse. Anticipate and avoid problems - or meet them head on at the outset. Overcome fear by attacking it.

Laugh Often
KEKICH'S CREDO #90

Find an excuse to laugh every chance you get, especially when you least feel like it.

Red Flag - "Trust Me"
KEKICH'S CREDO #91

When someone makes a big issue about his honesty or achievements, he is probably dishonest or a failure.

Compound Interest
KEKICH'S CREDO #92

Put the magic power of compound interest to work with every available dollar.

Invest In Yourself
KEKICH'S CREDO #93

The best investment you will ever make is your steady increase of knowledge. Invest in yourself. Thirty minutes of study per day eventually makes you an expert in any subject - but only if you apply that knowledge. Study alone is no substitute for experience. Education is always painfully slow.

What If This Was Published?
KEKICH'S CREDO #94

For each important action you take, ask yourself if you would be embarrassed if it were published. It takes a lifetime of effort to build a good reputation but only a moment of stupidity to destroy it.

You Are Your Thoughts
KEKICH'S CREDO #95

You are exactly what you believe and think about all day long. Constantly monitor your thoughts.

Be Skeptical
KEKICH'S CREDO #96

Skepticism is a key to rational thinking. Be especially skeptical of your own cherished beliefs. You might be wrong... and things change.

Kill Anxiety
KEKICH'S CREDO #97

Anxiety is usually caused by lack of control, organization, preparation, and action.

Use The Scientific Method
KEKICH'S CREDO #98

The first rule of sharpening your mind is to be an alert and sensitive observer. Assume nothing. If it can't be observed, it's not true. Never act on blind faith. Whenever something sounds too good to be true, it almost always is. Refuse to be swayed by emotion when it conflicts with reason. Observation is the genesis of all knowledge and progress... and is the first and last step of every thinking man's tool - The Scientific Method. All science and most progress is built on the Scientific Method (most non- scientists use it by accident).

The steps are:

1) OBSERVATION. Gathering and rationally organizing facts. This is where most people fail.

2) INDUCTIVE REASONING. Forming a hypothesis - or a generalization of facts held to be true.

3) EXTRAPOLATION. Making a projection or prediction based on the hypothesis in areas you didn't yet observe.

4) OBSERVATION. A test for the hypothesis to see if it works.

Learn and Profit Vicariously
KEKICH'S CREDO #99

Experience is not what happens to you. It's what you do with what happens to you. It takes a wise man to learn from his own mistakes... and a genius to learn and profit from the mistakes and experiences of others.

Reverse Death
KEKICH'S CREDO #100

The purpose of life is to delay, avoid and eventually reverse death.

Conclusion
100 Credos to Live By

As we have learned while reading Dave Kekich's 100 Credos, you can succeed best and quickest by helping others to succeed. This is the driving force behind why we created this book. We hope you have enjoyed reading these credos and continue to study and apply them in your life as well as share them with others who you care about. This book is the perfect gift to give the person who has everything as well as someone who doesn't.

To Purchase Additional Copies or See Bulk Order Pricing, Please Visit:

WeHelpAuthors.com/kekich-credos

Special Thanks To:

Dave Kekich

Joe Polish

Dr. Andrew J. Galambos

Dr. Wallace Ward

Frederick Mann

Dr. Craig C. McGraw

Daniel Sullivan

George S. Clason

Gary C. Halbert

Sir Isaac Newton

Peter Drucker

Brian Tracy

Winston Churchill

Napoleon Hill

Bobby Jones

Joe Paterno

John Paul DeJoria

Dr. Yul Brown

Patrick Malloy

Vince Lombardi

Thomas J. Peters

Harry Stottle

Jon Benson

Anonymous (all those wonderful insightful heroes who influenced me one way or another, either consciously or unconsciously, but whose names I can't attach to any particular Credo.)

Reviews

We truly hope you loved reading this book. It is a quick and easy read but do not discredit the knowledge and wisdom that Dave Kekich passed along to us. Put into practice, these Credo's can change both your business and your personal life!

We love 5 Star Reviews but only if they are legit. If this book moved you, helped you, or you just loved it, please take the time to let other's know.

To leave a review, please go to:

WeHelpAuthors.com/reviews/kekich-credos

Dave Kekich
Learn More

Dave was a great friend and a great contributor to human life and longevity. He helped with many advancements in health and science. He lived an incredible life, in spite of the fact that he was paralyzed from the chest down. To honor his life and legacy, we've created a tribute page where you can watch valuable presentations from Dave.

Dave Kekich

David A. Streen
Meet Dave

Dave loves helping people, especially authors and entrepreneurs.

His superpowers are strategic planning and marketing. These coupled with his unique ability to see the clearest path to the desired result has helped countless people turn their dreams into reality. Dave not only gets amazing results for his clients, he makes the process as fun and enjoyable as possible.

Dave Streen

DaveStreen.com

DavesBooks.com

DavesPodcasts.com

Someone like you wrote this book.

We helped.

If you've considered writing your own,
do not try to figure it out alone.

WeHelpAuthors takes you from idea to published author.

www.ingramcontent.com/pod-product-compliance
Lightning Source LLC
Chambersburg PA
CBHW071443130726
47997CB00006B/2213